12 Folk Songs
for Solo Singers

12 Folk Songs Arranged for Solo Voice and Piano...
For Recitals, Concerts, and Contests

COMPILED AND EDITED BY SALLY K. ALBRECHT

Contents

Alfred

Medium High Book (31044)	ISBN-10: 0-7390-5782-0	ISBN-13: 978-0-7390-5782-7
Medium High Accompaniment CD (31045)	ISBN-10: 0-7390-5783-9	ISBN-13: 978-0-7390-5783-4
Medium High Book & CD (31046)	ISBN-10: 0-7390-5760-X	ISBN-13: 978-0-7390-5760-5
Medium Low Book (31047)	ISBN-10: 0-7390-5784-7	ISBN-13: 978-0-7390-5784-1
Medium Low Accompaniment CD (31048)	ISBN-10: 0-7390-5785-5	ISBN-13: 978-0-7390-5785-8
Medium Low Book & CD (31049)	ISBN-10: 0-7390-5761-8	ISBN-13: 978-0-7390-5761-2

The solos in this collection are also available as Alfred choral arrangements.
Visit **alfred.com** for more information.

Cover art: *Farm Scene*, c. 1975
by Mattie Lou O'Kelley (American, 1908–1997)
Oil on canvas (24" x 36¼")
Smithsonian American Art Museum
Gift of Herbert Waide Hemphill. Jr., 1998.84.28

ABOUT THE COVER
Mattie Lou O'Kelley, a native of rural Georgia, began painting at the age of 60. Her memory paintings, often idyllic landscapes or farm scenes filled with people, animals, and perfectly shaped trees, depict her fondest memories of her childhood in Georgia. Ms. O'Kelley's early paintings were displayed in the museum shop at the High Museum of Art in Atlanta where they were discovered by Robert Bishop, Director of the American Museum of Folk Art. Her works are now included in the collections of many major museums.

1. A-ROVING

Sea Chanty
Arranged by **GARY E. PARKS**

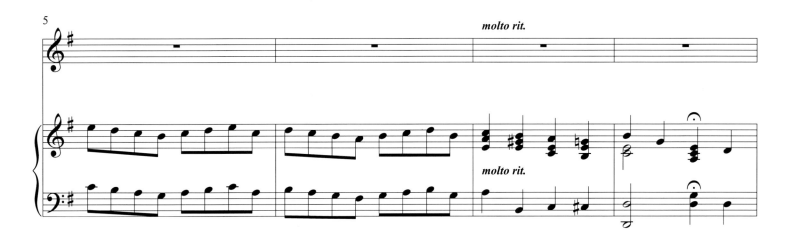

4

In Amster - dam I met a maid, mark well what I do say. In
Her lips were red, her eyes were brown, mark well what I do say. Her

In Amster - dam I met a maid a - stroll - ing on the prom - e - nade. I'll
Her lips were red, her eyes were brown, her hair was black and hang - ing down. I'll

go no more a - rov - ing with you fair maid. A -

rov - ing, a - rov - ing, since rov - ing's been my *ru - i - n. I'll

* pronounced "roo-eye-in"
31044

rov-ing's been my ru-i-n. I'll go no more a-rov-ing with you fair maid. I told the maid, quite hon-est-ly, I live up-on the sea. The sea is where I feel so free. She said, "A sail-or's not for me!" I'll go no more a-rov-ing with

2. ARIRANG

English text by
JONATHAN S. LIM *and* **SONJA POORMAN**

Korean Folk Song
Arranged by **SONJA POORMAN**

* Play notes in brackets only in absense of flute/C-instrument.
Separate part on page 15.

12

31044

14

PRONUNCIATION GUIDE

Arirang is the most well-known of all Korean folk songs, most of which are primarily based on the pentatonic (5-tone) scale. ARIRANG is the name of a Korean mountain located outside of Seoul.

A-ri-rang, A-ri-rang, a-ra-ri-yo,
Ah-ree-rahng, Ah-ree-rahng, ah-rah-ree-yoh,
(Arirang, Arirang, my love is leaving,)

A-ri-rang go-gay-roll no-mo gahn-da.
Ah-ree-rahng goh-geh-rohl noh-moh gahn-dah.
(He/she is going over the hill.)

Nah-roll bow-ri-go gah shi-non nie-mun
Nah-rohl bah-ree-goh gah shee-nohn nyee-moon
(The one who leaves me)

Shim-ri-do mo-ut-ga-so bahl-byeong nanh-da.
Sheem-ree-doh moh-oot-gah-soh bahl-beeyong nahn-dah.
(will not go far without hurting his/her feet.)

2. ARIRANG

FLUTE / C-INSTRUMENT

Korean Folk Song
Arranged by **SONJA POORMAN**

NOTE: The purchase of this book carries with it the right to photocopy this page.

3. BY WATERS CLEAR AND FLOWING

Appalachian Folk Song
Arranged, with new words and music, by
DOUGLAS E. WAGNER (ASCAP)

By wa - ters clear and flow - ing I

walked one day,_____ and thought a - bout my

34

clear,_____ when hand in hand u - nit - ed, we

37

walked to-geth - er here._____ But still my heart is

39

40

cheer - ful, as long as hope re - mains,_____ as

43

long as peace - ful wa - ters are there to ease the

4. HOW CAN I KEEP FROM SINGING?

American Folk Hymn
Arranged by **ANDY BECK**

though the tem - pest 'round me roars, I know the truth, it liv - eth.

What though the dark - ness 'round me close, songs in the night it

giv - eth._____ No

storm can shake my in - most calm, I hear the mu - sic ring - ing. It

5. JOHNNY'S GONE

(I Know Where I'm Going /Johnny Has Gone for a Soldier)

American Folk Songs
Arranged by **MARK HAYES** (ASCAP)

37
hand - some, win - some John - ny._____

42 **JOHNNY HAS GONE FOR A SOLDIER**

40
a tempo
Here I sit on But-ter-milk Hill,

44
Who could blame me, cry my fill; And ev-'ry tear would_____

47
turn a mill: John-ny has gone for a sol - dier.

31044

6. LAND OF OUR DREAMS

New words by **HOPE HARRISON**
Arranged by **JAY ALTHOUSE**

Based on an Armenian Lullaby
Adapted, with new music, by **HOPE HARRISON**

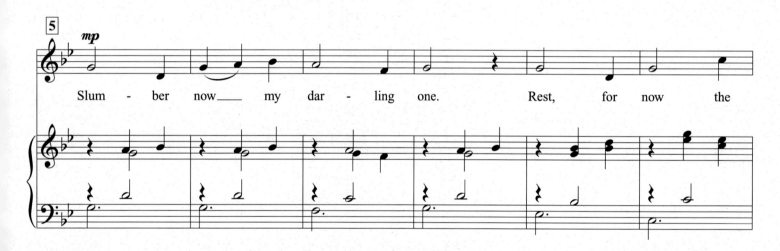

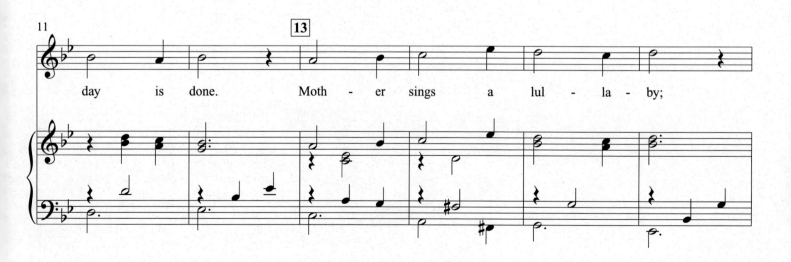

land of the free. Sail a-way, sail a-way to a home for my chil-dren.

Call-ing to you. Call-ing to me. Call-ing to you_____

and to me._____ Slum - ber

now___ my dar - ling one. We're off to the land of our dreams._____

7. THE LASS FROM THE LOW COUNTRY

English Folk Song
Arranged by **VICKI TUCKER COURTNEY** (ASCAP)

And she loved his lord - ship so ten - der - ly.

Oh, sor - row, deep sor - row.

Now she sleeps in the val - ley where the wild flow - ers

nod. And no one knows she loved him

but her-self_____ and____ God._____

One day when the snow was_____

on the mead,_____ he passed her_____ by on his

milk-white steed._____ She spoke to him low but he

If you be a lass from the low coun - try,_____ don't love an - y Lord of_____ high de - gree._____ He may have no feel - ing of sym - pa - thy._____ Oh, sor - row,_____ deep

sor - row._____ Now she sleeps in the val - ley where the

wild flow - ers nod. And no one knows_____ she loved him_____

_____ but her - self_____ and_____

God._____

8. OL' DAN TUCKER

American Folk Song
Arranged by
DAVE *and* **JEAN PERRY** (ASCAP)

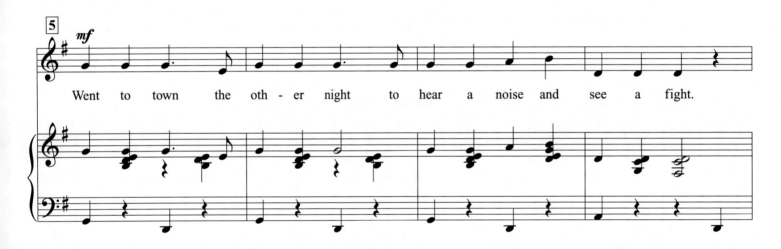

Went to town the oth - er night to hear a noise and see a fight.

All the peo - ple were run - nin' a - round, say - in', "Ol' Dan Tuck - er's come to town."

Ol' Dan,_____ Ol' Dan Tuck-er came to town,

rid-in' a bil-ly goat lead-in' a hound. Hound dog barked and the bil-ly goat jumped.

Threw Ol' Dan right on a stump. Oh_____

Get out the way, you're too late.

Get out the way, Ol' Dan Tuck - er. You're too late to come for sup - per.

Sup - per's o - ver and din - ner's cook - in'. Ol' Dan Tuck-er's just stand-in' there

look - in'.

Get out the way, Ol' Dan Tuck - er.

9. STAR OF THE COUNTY DOWN

Traditional, *alt. D.E.W.*

Irish Folk Song
Arranged by **DOUGLAS E. WAGNER** (ASCAP)

* English form of *boithrin* (a narrow country road).

10. SUN DON'T SET IN THE MORNIN'

Traditional Words, with new
verses by **JAY ALTHOUSE**

Based on a Southern Folk Hymn
Adapted and Arranged by **JAY ALTHOUSE**

11. WATERS RIPPLE AND FLOW

Words by **JAY ALTHOUSE**

Czecho-Slovak Folk Song
Arranged by **JAY ALTHOUSE**

Wa - ters rip-ple and flow_____ like an ev - er chang-ing sky.

Sea - sons come and they go; time is slow-ly pass-ing

flow - ing ev - er-more for me. Wa - ters rip - ple and

flow, flow - ing ev - er-more for me.

Wa - ters rip - ple and flow, flow - ing ev - er-more for

flow - ing ev - er - more for me. Wa - ters rip - ple and

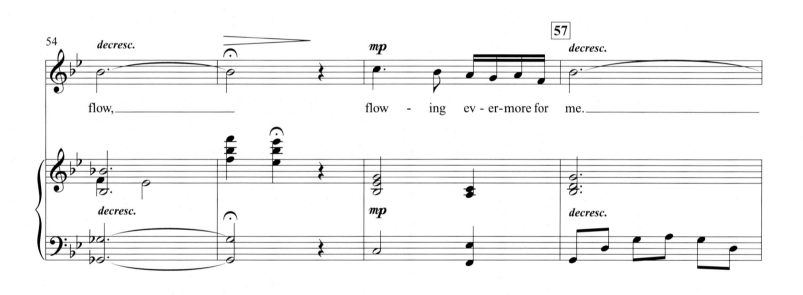

flow,_____ flow - ing ev - er - more for me._____

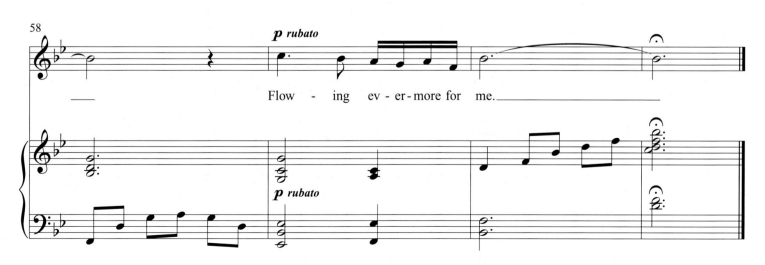

_____ Flow - ing ev - er - more for me._____

12. WHERE THE SEA MEETS THE SKY

Words and Music by
SALLY K. ALBRECHT